MEDITATIONS

IN TEN MINUTES A DAY

SIMPLE STOIC WISDOM FOR
CLARITY, CALM, AND COURAGE

MEDITATIONS

IN TEN MINUTES A DAY

Marcus Aurelius

Translation published in 1862 by George Long.

Reprint edition by Sound Wisdom, 2025

This book is a historical artifact. Sound Wisdom has reprinted this work to preserve and share the best wisdom handed down from great men and women in history. Not all of the ideas and beliefs held by these authors remain acceptable in our present time, and Sound Wisdom does not condone or endorse every belief shared within this book. We encourage readers to glean the best timeless wisdom from these pages, while exercising grace toward our ancestors' flaws and forgiveness toward the mistakes of the past.

ISBN 13: 978-1-64095-694-0

Ebook ISBN: 978-1-64095-695-7

1 2 3 4 5 6 7 8 / 29 28 27 26 25

Love the art, poor as it may be, which you have learned, and be content with it; and pass through the rest of life like one who has entrusted to the gods with his whole soul all that he has, making yourself neither the tyrant nor the slave of any man.

Marcus Aurelius, *Meditations*

CONTENTS

DAY 1

Begin the morning by saying to yourself, "I shall meet with the busybody, the ungrateful, arrogant, deceitful, envious, unsocial. They are that way because of their ignorance of good and evil. But I who have seen the nature of the good, that it is beautiful, and of the bad, that it is ugly, and the nature of him who does wrong, that it is akin to me—I can neither be injured by any of them, for no one can put upon me what is ugly, nor can I be angry with others nor hate them." For we are made for cooperation. To act against one another, then, is contrary to nature; and it is acting against one another to be vexed and to turn away (Book II: i).

Through the universal substance as through a furious torrent all bodies are carried, being by their nature united with and cooperating with the whole, as the parts of our body with one another (Book VII: xix).

Every duty is made up of certain parts. These it is your duty to observe, and without being disturbed or showing anger toward those who are angry with you, to go on your way and finish that which is set before you (Book VI: xxvi).

Consider how much more pain is brought on us by the anger and vexation caused by such acts than by the acts themselves, at which we are angry and vexed (Book XI: xviii).

People exist for the sake of one another. Teach them then, or bear with them (Book VIII: lix).

My Meditations

1. Where have I experienced frustration with other people in my professional and/or personal life?

2. What are the potential benefits to me if I adopt this attitude, even with frustrating people?

3. How can I practically implement this philosophy of patience and cooperation?

DAY 2

Remember how long you have been putting things off, and how often you have received an opportunity from the gods, and yet do not use it. You must now at last perceive that a limit of time is fixed for you, which if you do not use it for clearing away the clouds from your mind, it will go and you will go, and it will never return (Book II: iv).

Everything material soon disappears in the substance of the whole; and everything is very soon taken back into the universal reason; and the memory of everything is very soon overwhelmed in time (Book VII: x).

Though you should live three thousand years, remember that no one loses any other life than the one they now live, nor lives any other than the one they now lose. The longest and shortest are thus brought to the same. For the present is the same to all. A person cannot lose either the past or the future—for what you do not have, how can anyone take this from you? If it is true that the present is the only thing which you have, and that you cannot lose a thing you do not have, the present is the only thing of which you can be deprived (Book II: xiv).

Do not disturb yourself by thinking of the whole of your life. Let not your thoughts at once embrace all the various troubles which you may expect to befall you. Neither the future nor the past pains you, but only the present (Book VIII: xxxvi).

Since it is possible that you may depart from life this very moment, regulate every act and thought accordingly. Every person's life is sufficient (Book II: vi, xi).

My Meditations

1. Where have I wasted time in my professional and/or personal life?

2. What are the potential benefits to me if I focus on making the most of my time in the present?

3. How can I practically implement this proactive philosophy?

DAY 3

In the morning when you rise unwillingly, let this thought be present: I am rising to the work of a human being. Why then am I dissatisfied if I am going to do the things for which I exist and for which I was brought into the world? Or have I been made for this, to lie in the bedclothes and keep myself warm?

"But this is more pleasant."

Do you exist then to take your pleasure, and not at all for action or exertion? Do you not see the little plants, the little birds, the ants, the spiders, the bees working together to put in order their several parts of the universe? And are you unwilling to do the work of a human being, and do you not make haste to do that which is according to your nature?

"But it is necessary to take rest also."

It is necessary. However, Nature has fixed bounds to this too. She has fixed bounds to eating and drinking, and yet you go beyond these bounds, beyond what is sufficient; yet in your acts it is not so, but you stop short of what you can do. So you love not yourself, for if you did, you would love your nature and her will.

But those who love their several arts exhaust themselves in working at them unwashed and without food; but you value your own nature less than the turner values the turning art, or the dancer the dancing art, or the lover of money values his money, or the vain-glorious man his little glory. And such people, when they have a violent affection to a thing, choose neither to eat nor to sleep rather than to perfect the things which they care for. But are the acts which concern society more vile in your eyes and less worthy of your labor? (Book V: i)

No longer talk at all about the kind of person that a good person ought to be, but be such (Book X: xvi).

If it is not right, do not do it; if it is not true, do not say it (Book XII: xvii).

My Meditations

1. Where have I been tempted by laziness in my professional and/or personal life?

2. What are the potential benefits to me of emphasizing consistent integrity?

3. How can I practically implement this philosophy of honesty and self-discipline?

DAY 4

And virtue they will curse, speaking harsh words (Book XI: xxxii).

Nothing is more wretched than a person who seeks by conjecture what is in the minds of their neighbors, without perceiving that it is sufficient to attend to their own spirit within, and to reverence it sincerely. And reverence of the spirit consists in keeping it pure from passion and thoughtlessness and dissatisfaction (Book II: xiii).

When another blames you or hates you, or when people say about you anything injurious, approach their poor souls, penetrate within, and see what kind of people they are. You will discover that there is no reason to take any trouble that these people may have this or that opinion about you. However, you must be well disposed toward them, for by nature they are friends (Book IX: xxvii).

I have often wondered how it is that everyone loves themselves more than all the rest of humanity, but yet sets less value on their own opinion of themselves than on the opinions of others. So much more respect have we to what our neighbors will think of us than to what we will think of ourselves (Book XII: iv).

Socrates used to call the opinions of the many by the name of *Lamiae*—bugbears to frighten children (Book XI: xxiii).

My Meditations

1. Where have I been too concerned with the opinions of others in my professional and/or personal life?

2. What are the potential benefits to me if I focus on sticking to my own values, regardless of what others think?

3. How can I practically train myself to stop over-emphasizing what other people think?

DAY 5

Failing to see what is in the mind of another has seldom made a person unhappy; but those who do not observe the movements of their own minds will absolutely be unhappy (Book II: viii).

In the mind of one who is chastened and purified you will find no corrupt matter, nor impurity, nor any sore skinned over (Book III: viii).

Everywhere and at all times it is in your power piously to acquiesce in your present condition, and to behave justly to those who are about you, and to exert your skill upon your present thoughts, that nothing will steal into them without being well examined (Book VII: liv).

Look within. Within is the fountain of good, and it will ever bubble up, if you will ever dig (Book VII: lix).

The things are three of which you are composed: a little body, a little breath life, intelligence. Of these the first two are yours, so far as it is your duty to take care of them; but the third alone is properly yours. If you will separate from this ruling faculty the things which are attached to it by the impressions of sense, and the things of time to come and of time that is past, and if you shall strive to live only what is really your life, that is, the present—then you will be able to pass that portion of life which remains for you up to the time of your death free from perturbations, nobly, and obedient to your own spirit that is within you (Book XII: iii).

My Meditations

1. In what way have I made an effort to understand myself in my professional and/or personal life?

2. What are the potential benefits to me if I examine my own mind more closely?

3. How can I practically implement this philosophy of introspection and self-knowledge?

DAY 6

Everything which belongs to the body is a stream, and what belongs to the soul is a dream and vapor, and life is a warfare and a stranger's sojourn, and after fame is oblivion. But if there is no harm to the elements themselves when each continually change into another, why should a person have any apprehension about the change and dissolution of all the elements? For it is according to nature, and nothing is evil which is according to nature (Book II: xvii).

Everyone lives only this present time, which is an indivisible point, and that all the rest of their life is either past or it is uncertain. Short then is the time which everyone lives; and small the nook of the earth where they live; and short too the longest posthumous fame, and even this only continued by a succession of poor human beings, who will very soon die, and who know not even themselves, much less the one who died long ago (Book III: x).

Hippocrates, after curing many diseases, himself fell sick and died. The Chaldaei foretold the deaths of many, and then fate caught them too. Alexander and Pompeius, and Caius Caesar, after so often completely destroying whole cities, and in battle cutting to pieces many ten thousands of cavalry and infantry, themselves too at last departed from life. What means all this? You have embarked, you have made the voyage, you are come to shore; get out. If indeed to another life, there is no lack of gods; but if to a state without sensation, you will cease to be held by pains and pleasures, as a slave to the vessel (Book III: iii).

Near is your forgetfulness of all things; and near the forgetfulness of you by all (Book VII: xxi).

How many together with whom I came into the world are already gone out of it! (Book VI: lvi)

My Meditations

1. Do I live with an awareness that life is short? Or do I block out this idea and avoid facing my mortality?

2. What are the potential benefits to me and/or my family if I take a close look at how I'm living, with my own mortality in mind?

3. Are there practical things I need to do to remind myself that life is short? How can I adjust my schedule to make better use of my time?

DAY 7

The soul does violence to itself, first of all, when it becomes vexed at anything which happens. This is a separation of ourselves from nature, in some part of which the natures of all other things are contained.

In the next place, the soul does violence to itself when it turns away from anyone.

In the third place, the soul does violence to itself when it is overpowered by pleasure or by pain.

Fourth, when it plays a part, and does or says anything insincerely and untruly.

Fifth, when it allows any act of its own and any movement to be without an aim, and does anything thoughtlessly. Even the smallest things should be done with reference to an end; and the end of humans is to follow reason and the law (Book II: xvi).

The spherical form of the soul maintains its figure when it is neither extended toward any object, nor contracted inward, nor dispersed, nor sinks down, but is illuminated by light, by which it sees the truth—the truth of all things and the truth that is in itself (Book XI: xii).

Be you upright, or be made upright (Book VII: xii).

My Meditations

1. In my professional and/or personal life, have I harmed myself by any acts of "violence" toward my soul?

2. How have I worked against myself? How do I best care for myself?

3. How can I practically improve my own soul's health?

DAY 8

Nothing is more disgraceful than a wolfish and false friendship. Avoid this most of all. The good and simple and benevolent show all these things in the eyes, and there is no mistaking (Book XI: xv).

If one should suddenly ask, "What have you now in your thoughts?" with perfect openness you should be able to immediately answer, "This or that." From your words it should be plain that everything in you is simple and benevolent, and such as befits a social creature—one who cares not for thoughts about pleasure or sensual enjoyments at all, nor has any rivalry or envy and suspicion, or anything else which would make you blush if you had to admit that it was in your mind (Book III: iv).

Whatever anyone does or says, I must be good; just as if the gold, or the emerald, or the purple were always saying this. Whatever anyone does or says, I must be emerald and keep my color (Book VII: xv).

When you have assumed these names—good, modest, true, rational, a person of equanimity, and magnanimous—take care that you do not change these names; and if you should lose them, quickly return to them. Fix yourself in the possession of these few names; and if you are able to abide in them, abide as if you were removed to certain islands of the Happy (Book X: viii).

Speak appropriately both in the senate and to everyone, whoever they may be, not with any affectation. Use plain discourse (Book VIII: xxx).

My Meditations

1. Where have I experienced hypocrisy in my professional and/or personal life?

2. Have I been guilty of "being fake" in certain contexts?

3. How can I practically implement this philosophy of honesty and transparency?

DAY 9

When someone has done you any wrong, immediately consider with what opinion about good or evil they have done wrong. For when you have seen this, you will pity them, and will neither wonder nor be angry. For either you yourself think the same thing to be good that they do, or another thing of the same kind. It is your duty then to pardon them. But if you do not think such things to be good or evil, you will more readily be well disposed to one who is in error (Book VII: xxvi).

It is unique to humans to love even those who do wrong. And this happens, if when they do wrong it occurs to you that they are kinsmen, and that they do wrong through ignorance and unintentionally, and that soon both of you will die; and above all, that the wrongdoer has done you no harm, for they have not made your ruling faculty worse than it was before (Book VII: xxii).

Do not disturb yourself. Make yourself all simplicity. Does anyone do wrong? It is to themselves that they do the wrong. Has anything happened to you? Well—out of the universe from the beginning everything which happens has been apportioned and spun out to you. In a word, your life is short. You must turn to profit the present by the aid of reason and justice. Be sober in your relaxation (Book IV: xxvi).

It is your duty to leave another person's wrongful act there where it is (Book IX: xx).

The best way of avenging yourself is to not become like the wrongdoer (Book VI: vi).

My Meditations

1. Where have I experienced injustice in my professional and/or personal life?

2. What are the potential benefits to me if I forgive the wrongs done to me?

3. How can I practically implement this philosophy of forgiveness?

DAY 10

Constantly regard the universe as one living being, having one substance and one soul; and observe how all things have reference to one perception, the perception of this one living being; and how all things act with one movement; and how all things are the cooperating causes of all things which exist; observe too the continuous spinning of the thread and the contexture of the web (Book IV: xl).

That which does no harm to the state does no harm to the citizen. In the case of every appearance of harm apply this rule: if the state is not harmed by this, neither am I harmed (Book V: xxii).

As you yourself are a component part of a social system, so let every act of yours be a component part of social life. Whatever act of yours that has no reference either immediately or remotely to a social end, this tears asunder your life, and does not allow it to be one, and it is of the nature of a mutiny (Book IX: xxiii).

Take pleasure in one thing and rest in it, in passing from one social act to another social act, thinking of God (Book VI: vii).

That which is not good for the swarm, neither is it good for the bee (Book VI: liv).

My Meditations

1. How do I see my professional and/or personal life being influenced by the well-being of society around me?

2. What are the potential benefits to me of contributing to the good of the whole, of my community?

3. How can I practically influence my society in a positive way?

DAY 11

One who has a vehement desire for posthumous fame does not consider that all those who remember them will also die very soon; then again also they who have succeeded them, until the whole remembrance will have been extinguished as it is transmitted through people who foolishly admire and perish. But suppose that the remembrance will be immortal, what then is this to you? And I say not what is it to the dead, but what is it to the living? What is praise, except indeed so far as it has a certain utility? (Book IV: xix)

Perhaps the desire of the thing called fame will torment you. See how soon everything is forgotten, and look at the chaos of infinite time on each side of the present, and the emptiness of applause, and the changeableness and want of judgment in those who pretend to give praise, and the narrowness of the space within which it is circumscribed and be quiet at last. For the whole earth is a point, and how small a nook in it is this your dwelling, and how few are there in it, and what kind of people are they who will praise you (Book IV: iii).

How many after being celebrated by fame have been given up to oblivion; and how many who have celebrated the fame of others have long been dead? (Book VII: vi)

Do you wish to be praised by a person who curses themselves thrice every hour? Would you wish to please a person who does not please themselves? (Book VIII: liii)

Everything which is in any way beautiful is beautiful in itself, and terminates in itself, not having praise as part of itself. A thing is made neither worse nor better by being praised. That which is really beautiful has no need of anything; not more than law, not more than truth, not more than benevolence or modesty. Which of these things is beautiful because it is praised, or spoiled by being blamed? Is such a thing as an emerald made worse than it was, if it is not praised? (Book IV: xx)

My Meditations

1. Where have I placed too much value on the praise of others in my professional and/or personal life?

2. Do I sometimes do things a certain way for the sake of my reputation, rather than because it is what I really think is right?

3. What are some practical things I can do to help me identify unhealthy patterns of approval-seeking in my life?

DAY 12

Occupy yourself with few things, says the philosopher, if you would be tranquil. But consider if it would not be better to say, "Do what is necessary, and whatever the reason of the animal which is naturally social requires, and as it requires." For this brings not only the tranquility which comes from doing well, but also that which comes from doing few things. For the greatest part of what we say and do being unnecessary, if you take this away, you will have more leisure and less uneasiness. Accordingly, on every occasion you should ask yourself, "Is this one of the unnecessary things?" Take away not only unnecessary acts, but also unnecessary thoughts, for thus superfluous acts will not follow after (Book IV: xxiv).

Every moment think steadily to do what you have in hand with perfect and simple dignity, and give yourself relief from all other thoughts. Do every act of your life as if it were the last, laying aside all carelessness, hypocrisy, self-love, and discontent with the portion which has been given to you (Book II: v).

Do the external things which fall upon you distract you? Give yourself time to learn something new and good, and cease to be whirled around (Book II: vii).

I do my duty—other things trouble me not; for they are either things without life, or things without reason, or things that have rambled and know not the way (Book VI: xxii).

Let not future things disturb you, for you will come to them, if it will be necessary, having with you the same reason which now you use for present things (Book VII: viii).

My Meditations

1. Where have I been distracted or struggled with my priorities in my professional and/or personal life?

2. What are the potential benefits to me if I clean out distractions and focus on the present?

3. How can I practically implement this philosophy of prioritizing the present and not worrying about the uncertain future?

DAY 13

If you did ever see a hand cut off, or a foot, or a head, lying anywhere apart from the rest of the body, such does a person make themselves, as far as they can, who is not content with what happens, and separates themselves from others, or does anything unsocial. Suppose that you have detached yourself from the natural unity—for you were made by nature a part, but now you have cut yourself off—yet here there is this beautiful provision, that it is in your power again to unite yourself. God has allowed this to no other part, after it has been separated and cut asunder, to come together again. But consider the kindness by which he has distinguished humanity—it is in our power not to be separated at all from the universal; and when we have been separated, we are allowed to return and to be united and to resume our place as a part (Book VIII: xxxiv).

As the universe is made up out of all bodies to be such a body as it is, so out of all existing causes, destiny, of necessity, is made up to be such a cause as it is. Let us then receive these. Many prescriptions are disagreeable, but we accept them in the hope of health.

The integrity of the whole is mutilated if you cut off anything whatever from the conjunction and the continuity either of the parts or of the causes. And you do cut off, as far as it is in your power, when you are dissatisfied, and in a manner try to put anything out of the way (Book V: viii).

We are all working together to one end, some with knowledge and design, and others without knowing what they do. But people cooperate after different fashions. And even those cooperate abundantly who find fault with what happens and those who try to oppose it and to hinder it; for the universe had need even of such as these (Book VI: xlii).

A branch cut off from the adjacent branch must of necessity be cut off from the whole tree also. So too a person separated from another person has fallen off from the whole social community (Book XI: viii).

Adapt yourself to the things with which your lot has been cast—and the people among whom you have received your portion, love them, but do it truly sincerely (Book VI: xxxix).

My Meditations

1. Have I deprioritized my connections with people in my professional and/or personal life?

2. How has a lack of connection to other people harmed me?

3. How can I take practical steps to keep myself in healthy connections with other people?

DAY 14

Epicurus says, "In my sickness my conversation was not about my bodily sufferings, nor," says he, "did I talk on such subjects to those who visited me; but I continued to discourse on the nature of things as before, keeping to this main point, how the mind, while participating in such movements as go on in the poor flesh, will be free from perturbations and maintain its proper good. Nor did I," he says, "give the physicians an opportunity of putting on solemn looks, as if they were doing something great, but my life went on well and happily."

Do, then, the same that he did both in sickness, if you are sick, and in any other circumstances; for never to desert philosophy in any events that may befall us, nor to hold trifling talks either with an ignorant person or with one unacquainted with nature, is a principle of all schools of philosophy; but be intent only on that which you are now doing (Book IX: xli).

It is in your power whenever you shall choose to retire into yourself. For nowhere either with more quiet or more freedom from trouble does a person retire than into their own soul, particularly when they have within them such thoughts that by looking into them they are immediately in perfect tranquility; and I affirm that tranquility is nothing else than the good ordering of the mind. Constantly then give to yourself this retreat, and renew yourself; and let your principles be brief and fundamental (Book IV: iii).

The mind which is free from passions is a citadel, for a person has nothing more secure to which they can fly for refuge and for the future be inexpugnable (Book VIII: xlviii).

It is not right to vex ourselves at things, for they care nought about it (Book VII: xxxviii).

My Meditations

1. Where have I allowed circumstances to control my thinking?

2. What are the potential benefits to my professional and/or personal life if I could control my thoughts without being affected by day-to-day ups and downs?

3. How can I begin to take control of my thought life?

DAY 15

You are a little soul bearing about a corpse, as Epictetus used to say (Book IV: xli).

It is a vulgar, but still a useful help toward contempt of death, to pass in review those who have tenaciously stuck to life. What more then have they gained than those who have died early? Certainly they lie in their tombs somewhere at last. They have carried out many to be buried, and then were carried out themselves.

Altogether the interval is small between birth and death; and consider with how much trouble, and in company with what sort of people, and in what a feeble body, this interval is laboriously passed. Do not then consider life a thing of any value. For look to the immensity of time behind you, and to the time which is before you, another boundless space. In this infinity then what is the difference between one who lives three days and one who lives three generations? (Book IV: l)

Think of the universal substance, of which you have a very small portion; and of universal time, of which a short and indivisible interval has been assigned to you; and of that which is fixed by destiny, and how small a part of it you are (Book V: xxiv).

Time is like a river made up of the events which happen, and a violent stream; for as soon as a thing has been seen, it is carried away, and another comes in its place, and this will be carried away too (Book IV: xliii).

Short is the little which remains to you of life. Live as on a mountain. For it makes no difference whether you live there or here, if you live everywhere in the world (Book X: xv).

My Meditations

1. Do I take time regularly to remember the big picture?

2. How does this broad view change my perspective on the major issues I'm facing right now?

3. How can I adjust my framework to focus on what's really important?

DAY 16

Be like the promontory against which the waves continually break, but it stands firm and tames the fury of the water around it. Unhappy am I because this has happened to me? Not so, but happy am I, though this has happened to me, because I continue free from pain, neither crushed by the present nor fearing the future.

Well, you know the will of nature. Will then this which has happened prevent you from being just, magnanimous, temperate, prudent, secure against inconsiderate opinions and falsehood; will it prevent you from having modesty, freedom, and everything else, by the presence of which human nature obtains all that is its own? Remember too on every occasion which leads you to vexation to apply this principle—not that this is a misfortune, but that to bear it nobly is good fortune (Book IV: xlix).

Certainly, death and life, honor and dishonor, pain and pleasure—all these things equally happen to good people and bad, and they are things which make us neither better nor worse. Therefore they are neither good nor evil (Book II: xi).

Observe constantly that all things take place by change, and accustom yourself to consider that the nature of the universe loves nothing so much as to change the things which are and to make new things like them. For everything that exists is in a manner the seed of that which will be (Book IV: xxxvi).

Nothing happens to any person which they are not formed by nature to bear (Book V: xviii).

How have you behaved hitherto to the gods, your parents, brethren, children, teachers, to those who looked after your infancy, to your friends, kinsfolk, to your servants? Consider if you have hitherto behaved to all in such a way that this may be said of you, "Never have they wronged anyone in deed or word" (Book V: xxxi).

My Meditations

1. Have I ever demonstrated this kind of calm acceptance in my professional and/or personal life?

2. What are the potential benefits to me, my family, and my community if I view misfortunes and struggles this way?

3. What aspects of this stoic worldview appeal to me most? How can I practically implement them in my life?

DAY 17

The person who is honest and good ought to be exactly like a man who smells strong, so that the bystander as soon as they come near him must smell him, whether they choose or not (Book XI: xv).

How unsound and insincere is one who says, "I have determined to deal with you in a fair way"! What are you doing? There is no occasion to give this notice. It will soon show itself by acts. The voice ought to be plainly written on the forehead (Book XI: xv).

Never value anything as profitable which will compel you to break your promise, to lose your self-respect, to hate anyone, to suspect, to curse, to act the hypocrite, to desire anything which needs walls and curtains (Book III: vii).

Does another do me wrong? Let them look to it. They have their own disposition, their own activity. I now have what the universal nature now wills me to have; and I do what my nature now wills me to do (Book V: xxv).

You should consider it among the most absurd of things for a person not to speak from their real thoughts (Book XI: xix).

My Meditations

1. Where have I experienced insincerity in my professional and/or personal life?

2. What are the potential benefits to me of being so honest that people can't help but notice?

3. How can I practically implement this philosophy of thoroughly honest sincerity?

DAY 18

How many pleasures have been enjoyed by robbers, patricides, tyrants! (Book VI: xxxiv)

Let the part of your soul which leads and governs be undisturbed by the movements in the flesh, whether of pleasure or of pain; and let it not unite with them, but let it circumscribe itself and limit those affects to their parts (Book V: xxvi).

The one who loves fame considers another person's activity to be their own good; and one who loves pleasure, their own sensations; but one who has understanding considers their own acts to be their own good (Book VI: li).

Show those qualities then which are altogether in your power—sincerity, gravity, endurance of labor, aversion to pleasure, contentment with your portion and with few things, benevolence, frankness, no love of superfluity, freedom from trifling, magnanimity.

Do you not see how many qualities you are immediately able to exhibit, in which there is no excuse of natural incapacity and unfitness, and yet you still remain voluntarily below the mark? Or are you compelled through being defectively furnished by nature to murmur, and to be stingy, and to flatter, and to find fault with your poor body, and to try to please men, and to make great display, and to be so restless in your mind? No, by the gods; but you might have been delivered from these things long ago (Book V: v).

Body, soul, intelligence—to the body belong sensations, to the soul appetites, to the intelligence principles. To receive the impressions of forms by means of appearances belongs even to animals; to be pulled by the strings of desire belongs both to wild beasts and to tyrants (Book III: xvi).

My Meditations

1. Living in a culture that emphasizes the physical life, have I sacrificed intangible good for the sake of physical pleasure or comfort?

2. What are the potential benefits to me if I put mental or emotional gains above temporary physical enjoyment?

3. How can I practically implement this stoic belief in the value of the human soul above the body?

DAY 19

If anyone is able to convince me and show me that I do not think or act right, I will gladly change; for I seek the truth, by which no one was ever injured. But the person is injured who abides in error and ignorance (Book VI: xxi).

Have these two rules in readiness: do only whatever reason suggests for the use of others; and change your opinion, if there is any one at hand who sets you right. But this change of opinion must proceed only from a certain persuasion, as of what is just or of common advantage, not because it appears pleasant or brings reputation (Book IV: xii).

On the occasion of every act ask yourself, "How is this with respect to me? Will I repent of it? A little time and I am dead, and all is gone. What more do I seek, if what I am now doing is the work of an intelligent living being, and a social being, and one who is under the same law with God?" (Book VIII: ii)

Suppose any person will despise me. Let them look to that themselves. But I will look to this, that I be not discovered doing or saying anything deserving of contempt. For what evil is it to you, if you are now doing what is agreeable to your own nature, and are satisfied with that which at this moment is suitable to the nature of the universe? (Book XI: xiii)

What need is there of suspicious fear, since it is in your power to inquire what ought to be done? And if you see clear, go by this way content, without turning back; but if you do not see clear, stop and take the best advisers (Book X: xii).

My Meditations

1. In my professional and/or personal life, whose advice has been wise and invaluable to me, and whose input have I needed to reject because it disagrees with my values?

2. What are the consequences of refusing good advice or caving in to negative pressures?

3. How can I practically implement a strategy to help me distinguish between good and helpful counsel and the kind of damaging input I should reject?

DAY 20

A man deposits seed in a womb and goes away, and then another cause takes it and labors on it, and makes a child. What a thing from such a material! Again, the child passes food down through the throat, and then another cause takes it and makes perception and motion, and in fine, life and strength and other things; how many and how strange! Observe then the things which are produced in such a hidden way, and see the power, just as we see the power which carries things downward and upward, not with the eyes, but still no less plainly (Book X: xxvi).

You will neither do anything well which pertains to humankind without at the same time having a reference to things divine; nor the contrary (Book III: xiii).

Consider that everything which happens, happens justly, and if you observe carefully, you will find it to be so. Observe then as you have begun; and whatever you do, do it in conjunction with this—the being good, and in the sense in which a person is properly understood to be good. Keep to this in every action (Book IV: x).

If souls continue to exist, how does the air contain them from eternity? But how does the earth contain the bodies of those who have been buried from time so remote? For as here the mutation of these bodies after a certain continuance, whatever it may be, and their dissolution, make room for other dead bodies, so the souls which are removed into the air after subsisting for some time are transmuted and diffused, and assume a fiery nature by being received into the seminal intelligence of the universe, and in this way make room for the fresh souls which come to dwell there (Book IV: xxi).

A prayer of the Athenians: Rain, rain, O dear Zeus, down on the ploughed fields of the Athenians and on the plains. In truth we ought not to pray at all, or we ought to pray in this simple and noble fashion (Book V: vii).

My Meditations

1. How do I relate to the things I don't understand? Do I have a strong sense of faith in an unseen reality?

2. What is the benefit of believing in God? Does a belief in a divine world motivate me with a sense of accountability for my choices in this life?

3. In what way am I guided in daily life by my beliefs about things beyond my control or understanding?

DAY 21

War, astonishment, torpor, slavery will daily wipe out those holy principles of yours (Book X: ix).

Be not disgusted, nor discouraged, nor dissatisfied, if you do not succeed in doing everything according to right principles, but when you have failed, return back again, and be content if the greater part of what you do is consistent with human nature, and love this to which you return.

What is more agreeable than wisdom itself, when you think of the security and the happy course of all things which depend on the faculty of understanding and knowledge? (Book V: ix)

When you have been compelled by circumstances to be disturbed in a manner, quickly return to yourself, and do not continue out of tune longer than the compulsion lasts; for you will have more mastery over the harmony by continually recurring to it (Book VI: xi).

How can our principles become dead, unless the impressions and thoughts which correspond to them are extinguished? But it is in your power continuously to fan these thoughts into a flame. To recover your life is in your power (Book VII: ii).

In the application of your principles you must be like the martial artist, not like the gladiator; for the gladiator drops the sword which he uses and is killed; but the other always has his hand, and needs to do nothing else than use it (Book XII: ix).

My Meditations

1. When have I failed to do something I set out to do in my professional and/or personal life?

2. When have I come back and tried again after a failure? What did I gain from that?

3. How can I remind myself in a concrete way to "try, try again" after a defeat or failure?

DAY 22

What more do you want when you have done someone a service? Are you not content that you have done something conformable to your nature, and do you seek to be paid for it? Just as if the eye demanded a recompense for seeing, or the feet for walking (Book IX: xlii).

Have I done something for the general interest? Well then, I have had my reward. Let this always be present to your mind, and never stop doing such good (Book XI: iv).

When you have done a good act and another has received it, why do you still look for a third thing besides these, as fools do, either to have the reputation of having done a good act or to obtain a return? (Book VII: lxxiii)

Try how the life of the good person suits you, the life of one who is satisfied with their portion out of the whole, and satisfied with their own just acts and benevolent disposition (Book IV: xxv).

Humans are formed by nature to acts of benevolence. When they have done anything benevolent or in any other way conducive to the common interest, they have acted conformably to their constitution, and they get what is their own (Book IX: xlii).

My Meditations

1. Do I expect to be rewarded when I do something good in my professional and/or personal life?
2. How often do I act generously and helpfully toward others without even thinking about getting a reward for it?
3. How can I cultivate a benevolent nature and learn to be satisfied with my own good actions, even if they go totally unnoticed?

DAY 23

How much trouble you avoid if you do not look to see what your neighbor says or does or thinks, but only to what you do yourself, that it may be just and pure. Look not round at the depraved morals of others, but run straight along the line without deviating from it (Book IV: xviii).

Do not be whirled about, but in every movement have respect to justice, and on the occasion of every impression maintain the faculty of comprehension or understanding (Book IV: xxii).

If you find in human life anything better than justice, truth, temperance, fortitude, and, in a word, anything better than your own mind's self-satisfaction in the things which it enables you to do according to right reason—turn to it with all your soul, and enjoy that which you have found to be the best. But if nothing appears to be better than the Deity which is planted in you, if you find everything else smaller and of less value than this, give place to nothing else. If you do once diverge and incline to it, you will no longer be able to give the preference to that good thing which is your proper possession and your own. Do you, I say, simply and freely choose the better, and hold to it (Book III: vi).

If a person is mistaken, instruct them kindly and show them their error. But if you are not able, blame yourself, or blame not even yourself (Book X: iv).

Consider that people will do the same things anyway, even though you should burst (Book VIII: iv).

My Meditations

1. Where in my professional and/or personal life have other people pressured me to compromise my values?

2. What are the benefits for me if I set clear moral boundaries for myself?

3. Do I allow others too much influence in my life? How can I change that?

DAY 24

Think not so much of what you have not as of what you have. At the same time, however, take care that you do not through being so pleased with them accustom yourself to overvalue them, so as to be disturbed if ever you should not have them (Book VII: xxvii).

Everything is only for a day, both that which remembers and that which is remembered (Book IV: xxxv).

Things themselves touch not the soul, not in the least degree; nor have they admission to the soul, nor can they turn or move the soul. But the soul turns and moves itself alone, and whatever judgments it may think proper to make, such it makes for itself the things which present themselves to it (Book V: xix).

If the things do not come to you, the pursuits and avoidances of which disturb you, still in a manner you go to them. Let then your judgment about them be at rest, and they will remain quiet, and you will not be seen either pursuing or avoiding (Book XI: xi).

Receive wealth or prosperity without arrogance; and be ready to let it go (Book VIII: xxxiii).

My Meditations

1. Have I pursued material gains too much in my professional and/or personal life?
2. How high do I rank the material things I value, and how do they compare to a strong character?
3. How long will my valued possessions last? Until what date? How long will my most valuable character traits last?

DAY 25

A good disposition is invincible if it be genuine, and not an affected smile and acting a part (Book XI: xviii).

One who does not always have one and the same object in life cannot be one and the same all through their life. Make all your acts alike, and thus always be the same (Book XI: xxi).

Neither in writing nor in reading will you be able to lay down rules for others before you shall have first learned to obey rules yourself (Book XI: xxix).

One thing here is worth a great deal, to pass your life in truth and justice, with a benevolent disposition even to liars and unjust men (Book VI: xlvii).

The pride which is proud of its want of pride is the most intolerable of all (Book XII: xxvii).

My Meditations

1. Who in my professional and/or personal life is the most honest, genuine, and consistent in their character?
2. How do they benefit from their integrity? How do I compare to that standard?
3. What do they do that impresses me the most? How can I make that action my special goal, as a first step to becoming a more genuine person?

DAY 26

If a thing is difficult to be accomplished by yourself, do not think that it is impossible for a human. But if anything is possible for a human being and conformable to their nature, think that this can be attained by yourself too (Book VI: xix).

Does the sun undertake to do the work of the rain? And how is it with respect to each of the stars—are they not different and yet they work together to the same end? (Book VI: xliii)

If sailors abused the helmsman, or the sick the doctor, would they listen to anybody else? Or how could the helmsman secure the safety of those in the ship, or the doctor the health of those whom he attends? (Book VI: lv)

What does the work of a fig tree is a fig tree, and what does the work of a dog is a dog, and what does the work of a bee is a bee, and what does the work of a human is a human (Book X: viii).

Is my understanding sufficient for this or not? If it is sufficient, I use it for the work as an instrument given by the universal nature. But if it is not sufficient, then either I retire from the work and give way to the one who is able to do it better; or I do it as well as I can, taking to help me the one who can do what is now fit and useful for the general good (Book VII: v).

Neither the labor which the hand does nor that of the foot is contrary to nature, so long as the foot does the foot's work and the hand the hand's (Book VI: xxxiii).

My Meditations

1. Where have I experienced great teamwork and cooperation in my professional and/or personal life?

2. What are the potential benefits to me if I focus my efforts on collaboration?

3. How can I practically implement this philosophy of human interdependence? Where do I need to take a step back from trying to "do it all" myself?

DAY 27

The healthy eye ought to see all visible things and not to say, “I wish for green things,” for this is the condition of a diseased eye. And the healthy hearing and smelling ought to be ready to perceive all that can be heard and smelled. And the healthy stomach ought to be with respect to all food just as the mill with respect to all things which it is formed to grind (Book X: xxxv).

If you are pained by any external thing, it is not this thing that disturbs you, but your own judgment about it. And it is in your power to wipe out this judgment now (Book VIII: xlvii).

Everything harmonizes with me, which is harmonious to you, O Universe. Nothing for me is too early nor too late, which is in due time for you. Everything is fruit to me which your seasons bring, O Nature: from you are all things, in you are all things, to you all things return (Book IV: xxiii).

Many grains of frankincense on the same altar: one falls before, another falls after; but it makes no difference (Book IV: xv).

"A cucumber is bitter." Throw it away. "There are briers in the road." Turn aside from them. This is enough. Do not add, "And why were such things made in the world?" (Book VIII: l)

To nature who gives and takes back all, the one who is instructed and modest says, "Give what you will; take back what you will." And they say this not proudly, but obediently, and well pleased with her (Book X: xiv).

My Meditations

1. When in my professional and/or personal life have I been faced with undeniable realities that are hard to accept?

2. What are the potential benefits to me of choosing to accept the things I cannot change, even if they are unpleasant or evil?

3. How can I practically implement this philosophy of inner peace?

DAY 28

The Lacespiritians at their public spectacles used to set seats in the shade for strangers, but themselves sat down anywhere (Book XI: xxiv).

"The earth loves the shower" and "the solemn ether loves" and the universe loves to make whatever is about to be. I say then to the universe that I love as you love (Book X: xxi).

How cruel it is not to allow people to strive after the things which appear to them to be suitable to their nature and profitable! And yet in a manner you do not allow them to do this when you are vexed because they do wrong. For they are certainly moved toward things because they suppose them to be suitable to their nature and profitable to them. "But it is not so." Teach them, then, and show them without being angry (Book VI: xxvii).

Do not be carried along inconsiderately by the appearance of things, but give help to all according to your ability and their fitness (Book V: xxxvi).

It is your duty to show good humor and not a proud air; to understand that everyone is worth just so much as the things are worth about which they busy themselves (Book VII: iii).

My Meditations

1. Where have I experienced kindness and consideration the most in my professional and/or personal life?

2. What are the potential benefits to me if I demonstrate such kindness to others, even if they are difficult?

3. How can I practically implement this philosophy of preferring and caring for other people?

DAY 29

To seek what is impossible is madness—and it is impossible that the bad should not do something of this kind (Book V: xvii).

It is a ridiculous thing for a man not to fly from his own badness, which is indeed possible, but to fly from other men's badness, which is impossible (Book VII: lxxi).

Remember that as it is a shame to be surprised if the fig tree produces figs, so it is to be surprised if the world produces such and such things of which it is productive; and for the physician and the helmsman it is a shame to be surprised if a man has a fever, or if the wind is unfavorable (Book VIII: xv).

What is badness? It is that which you have often seen. Everywhere up and down you will find the same things, with which the old histories are filled, those of the middle ages and those of our own day—with which cities and houses are filled now. There is nothing new. All things are both familiar and short-lived (Book VII: i).

To expect bad people not to do wrong is madness, for anyone who expects this desires an impossibility. But to allow people to behave so to others, and to expect them not to do you any wrong, is irrational and tyrannical (Book XI: xviii).

My Meditations

1. Where have I experienced the dark side of humanity in my professional and/or personal life?

2. Do I tend to become cynical, expecting the worst from people, or do I tend toward gullibility—always being shocked when people mistreat me?

3. How can I train my thinking better, so that I am not shocked by bad behavior, but I also avoid cynicism?

DAY 30

Do not act as if you were going to live ten thousand years. Death hangs over you. While you live, while it is in your power, be good (Book IV: xvii).

On the occasion of everything that you do, pause and ask yourself if death is a dreadful thing because it deprives you of this (Book X: xxix).

There is no one so fortunate that there will not be by them when they are dying some who are pleased with what is going to happen. Suppose that they were a good and wise person, will there not be at least someone to say, "Let us at last breathe freely, being relieved from this schoolmaster. It is true that they were harsh to none of us, but I perceive that they tacitly condemn us." This is what is said of a good person. You will depart more contentedly by reflecting thus: "I am going away from such a life, in which even my associates in behalf of whom I have striven so much, prayed, and cared, themselves wish me to depart, hoping perchance to get some little advantage by it" (Book X: xxxvi).

The termination of life for every person is no evil, because neither is it shameful, since it is both independent of the will and not opposed to the general interest, but it is good, since it is seasonable, and profitable to and congruent with the universe (Book XII: xxiii).

Look at everything that exists, and observe that it is already in dissolution and in change, and as it were putrefaction or dispersion, or that everything is so constituted by nature as to die (Book X: xviii).

As the heaps of sand piled on one another hide the former sands; so in life the events which go before are soon covered by those which come after (Book VII: xxxiv).

My Meditations

1. Have I taken the time to consider death as a part of nature?

2. What are the potential benefits to me if I can come to see my own eventual death as a natural thing?

3. How can I train my thinking to overcome the fear of death?

DAY 31

You can pass your life in an equable flow of happiness if you can go by the right way, and think and act in the right way. These two things are common both to the soul of God and to the soul of every rational being—not to be hindered by another; and to hold good to consist in the disposition to justice and the practice of it, and in this to let your desire find its termination (Book V: xxxiv).

Within ten days you will seem a god to those to whom you are now a beast and an ape, if you will return to your principles and the worship of reason (Book IV: xvi).

A scowling look is altogether unnatural; when it is often assumed, the result is that all comeliness dies away, and at last is so completely extinguished that it cannot be again lighted up at all (Book VII: xxiv).

Practice yourself even in the things which you despair of accomplishing. For even the left hand, which is ineffectual for all other things for want of practice, holds the bridle more vigorously than the right hand; for it has been practiced in this (Book XII: vi).

My Meditations

1. What have I accomplished in my professional and/or personal life for which I had to try again and again before I succeeded?

2. What are the potential benefits to me of making an effort over and over to form a new habit?

3. How can I practically implement this philosophy of strengthening good habits through persistence?

DAY 32

Take away your opinion, and then there is taken away the complaint, "I have been harmed." Take away the complaint, "I have been harmed," and the harm is taken away (Book IV: vii).

Judge every word and deed which is according to nature to be fit for you; and be not diverted by the blame which follows from any people, nor by their words, but if a thing is good to be done or said, do not consider it unworthy of you (Book V: iii).

Retire into yourself. The rational principle which rules has this nature, that it is content with itself when it does what is just, and so secures tranquility (Book VII: xxviii).

How easy it is to repel and to wipe away every impression which is troublesome or unsuitable, and immediately to be in all tranquility (Book V: ii).

It is in my power never to act contrary to my god and spirit: for there is no one who will compel me to this (Book V: x).

My Meditations

1. Where have I struggled in my professional and/or personal life to resist the push and pull of others' opinions?

2. What are the potential benefits to me if I can get rid of self-doubt caused by naysayers?

3. How can I practically implement this philosophy of confidence in myself and my own values?

DAY 33

As a horse when he has run, a dog when he has tackled the game, a bee when it has made the honey, so a person who done a good act does not call out for others to come and see, but goes on to another act, as a vine goes on to produce again the grapes in season (Book V: vi).

Labor not unwillingly, nor without regard to the common interest, nor without due consideration, nor with distraction; be not either a person of many words, or busy about too many things. Be cheerful also, and seek not external help nor the tranquility which others give. A person must stand erect, not be kept erect by others (Book III: v).

If you have despaired of becoming a dialectician and skilled in the knowledge of nature, do not for this reason renounce the hope of being both free and modest, and social and obedient to God (Book VII: lxvii).

Adorn yourself with simplicity and modesty, and with indifference toward the things which lie between virtue and vice. Love humankind. Follow God. The poet says that law rules all, and it is enough to remember that law rules all (Book VII: xxxi).

Let no act be done without a purpose, nor otherwise than according to the perfect principles of art (Book IV: ii).

My Meditations

1. In my professional and/or personal life, have I made the right choices out of a desire for reward, or simply because I know it's the right thing to do?

2. What are the potential benefits to me of doing good for others without any thought of my own gain?

3. How can I practically implement this philosophy of selflessness and doing good for its own sake?

DAY 34

Unless I think that what has happened is an evil, I am not injured. And it is in my power not to think so (Book VII: xiv).

Wipe out the imagination; check desire; extinguish appetite; keep the ruling faculty in its own power. Stop the pulling of the strings. Confine yourself to the present. Let the wrong which is done by a person stay there where the wrong was done (Book VII: xxix; IX: vii).

In one way an arrow moves, in another way the mind. The mind indeed, both when it exercises caution and when it is employed about inquiry, moves straight onward not the less, and to its object (Book VIII: lx).

To the rational being the same act is according to nature and according to reason (Book VII: xi).

Consider that everything is opinion, and opinion is in your power. When you choose, take away your opinion, and like a mariner who has sailed around the cliff, you will find a calm, stable, and waveless bay (Book XII: xxii).

My Meditations

1. Have I experienced conflicts between emotions and reason in my professional and/or personal life?

2. What are the potential benefits to me if I weigh my decisions rationally, without being influenced by emotional reactions?

3. How can I practically implement this philosophy of following reason first and foremost?

DAY 35

Accustom yourself as much as possible on the occasion of anything being done by any person to inquire with yourself, "For what object is this person doing this?" But begin with yourself, and examine yourself first (Book X: xxxvii).

Examine people's ruling principles, even those of the wise, what kind of things they avoid, and what kind they pursue. Penetrate inward into people's leading principles, and you will see what judges you are afraid of, and what kind of judges they are of themselves (Book IV: xxxviii; IX: xviii).

Where there are things which appear most worthy of our approbation, we ought to lay them bare and look at their worthlessness and strip them of all the words by which they are exalted. For outward show is a wonderful perverter of the reason, and when you are most sure that you are employed about things worth your pains, it is then that it cheats you most (Book VI: xiii).

The reason which governs knows what its own disposition is, and what it does, and on what material it works (Book VI: v).

Look within. Let neither the peculiar quality of anything nor its value escape you (Book VI: iii).

My Meditations

1. In my professional and/or personal life, where have I examined people's inner motivations most carefully?

2. Do I scrutinize my own motivations? What are the potential benefits to me if I do so?

3. How can I practically implement this philosophy of looking beyond the surface?

DAY 36

Some things are hurrying into existence, and others are hurrying out of it; and of that which is coming into existence part is already extinguished. Motions and changes are continually renewing the world, just as the uninterrupted course of time is always renewing the infinite duration of ages. In this flowing stream then, on which there is no abiding, what is there of the things which hurry by on which a man would set a high price? It would be just as if a person should fall in love with one of the sparrows which fly by, but it has already passed out of sight (Book VI: xv).

How quickly all things disappear—in the universe the bodies themselves, but in time the remembrance of them. It is the part of the intellectual faculty to observe all things. To observe, too, what death is, and the fact that it is nothing else than an operation of nature; and if anyone is afraid of an operation of nature, they are a child (Book II: xii).

Often think of the rapidity with which things pass by and disappear, both the things which are and the things which are produced. For substance is like a river in a continual flow, and the activities of things are in constant change, and the causes work in infinite varieties; and there is hardly anything which stands still (Book V: xxiii).

Is anyone afraid of change? Why, what can take place without change? What then is more pleasing or more suitable to the universal nature? And can you take a bath unless the water undergoes a change? And can you be nourished unless the food undergoes a change? And can anything else that is useful be accomplished without change? Do you not see then that for yourself also to change is just the same, and equally necessary for the universal nature? (Book VII: xviii)

All existing things soon change, and they will either be reduced to vapor, if indeed all substance is one, or they will be dispersed (Book VI: iv).

My Meditations

1. Where have I experienced seasons of major change in my professional and/or personal life?

2. Do I fear or resist change? What are the potential benefits to me of living in an awareness of how temporary all thing are?

3. How can I practically implement this philosophy and experience contentment even in the face of uncomfortable changes?

DAY 37

To have contemplated human life for forty years is the same as to have contemplated it for ten thousand years. For what more will you see? (Book VII: xlix)

Consider the times of Vespasian. You will see all these things—people marrying, bringing up children, sick, dying, warring, feasting, trading, cultivating the ground, flattering, obstinately arrogant, suspecting, plotting, wishing for some to die, grumbling about the present, loving, heaping up treasure, desiring consulship, kingly power. Well, then, that life of these people no longer exists at all. Again, remove to the times of Trajan. Again, all is the same. Their life too is gone. See how many, after great efforts, soon fell and were resolved into the elements. Herein it is necessary to remember that the attention given to everything has its proper value and proportion. For thus you will not be dissatisfied, if you apply yourself to smaller matters no further than is fit (Book IV: xxxii).

Everything which happens is as familiar and well known as the rose in spring and the fruit in summer; for such is disease, and death, and slander, and treachery, and whatever else delights fools or vexes them (Book IV: xliv).

All things are the same, familiar in experience, and ephemeral in time, and worthless in the matter. Everything now is just as it was in the time of those whom we have buried (Book IX: xiv).

One who has seen present things has seen all, both everything which has taken place from all eternity and everything which will be for time without end; for all things are of one kin and of one form (Book VI: xxxvii).

My Meditations

1. Where have I experienced the maxim, "The more things change, the more they stay the same," in my professional and/or personal life?

2. Do I tend to get caught up in anything that seems new and fresh? What are the potential benefits to me of viewing life as essentially an unchanging cycle?

3. How can I practically implement this philosophical stoicism about apparent "novelties"?

DAY 38

It is a shame for the soul to be first to give way in this life, when your body does not give way (Book VI: xxix).

About what am I now employing my own soul? On every occasion I must ask myself this question, and inquire, "What have I now in this part of me which they call the ruling principle? And whose soul have I now—that of a child, or of a young man, or of a feeble person, or of a tyrant, or of a domestic animal, or of a wild beast?" (Book V: xi)

In contemplating yourself never include the vessel which surrounds you and these instruments which are attached about it. For they are like to an axe, differing only in this, that they grow to the body. For indeed there is no more use in these parts without the cause which moves and checks them than in the weaver's shuttle, and the writer's pen, and the driver's whip (Book X: xxxviii).

Does the light of the lamp shine without losing its splendor until it is extinguished? And will the truth which is in you and justice and temperance be extinguished before your death? (Book XII: xv)

My Meditations

1. Do I pay attention to my own soul as a daily part of my professional and/or personal life?

2. What external benefits might arise from a healthier interior life?

3. How can I practically implement this philosophy of soul enrichment?

DAY 39

As it happens to you in the amphitheater and such places, that the continual sight of the same things, and the uniformity, make the spectacle wearisome, so it is in the whole of life; for all things above, below, are the same and from the same (Book VI: xlvi).

Nature which governs the whole will soon change all things you see, and out of their substance will make other things, and again other things from the substance of them, in order that the world may be ever new (Book VII: xxv).

All things are changing, and you yourself are in continuous mutation and in a manner in continuous destruction, and the whole universe too (Book IX: xix).

Consider that before long you will be nobody and nowhere, nor will any of the things exist which you now see, nor any of those who are now living. For all things are formed by nature to change and be turned and to perish, in order that other things in continuous succession may exist (Book XII: xxi).

It is no evil for things to undergo change, and no good for things to subsist in consequence of change (Book IV: xlii).

My Meditations

1. Where have I experienced growth in my professional and/or personal life?
2. What are the potential benefits to me if I seek progress in areas that may have been stagnant for a while?
3. How can I practically implement this philosophy of continuous evolution?

DAY 40

All things are implicated with one another, and the bond is holy; and there is hardly anything unconnected with any other thing. For there is one universe made up of all things, and one god who pervades all things, and one substance, and one law, one common reason in all intelligent animals, and one truth (Book VII: ix).

The intelligence of the universe is social. Accordingly it has made the inferior things for the sake of the superior, and it has fitted the superior to one another. You see how it has subordinated, coordinated, and assigned to everything its proper portion, and has brought together into concord with one another the things which are the best (Book V: xxx).

In one respect humanity is the nearest thing to me, so far as I must do good to others and endure them. But so far as some people make themselves obstacles to my proper acts, they become to me one of the things which are indifferent, no less than the sun or wind or a wild beast. Now it is true that these may impede my action, but they are no impediments to my affects and disposition. For the mind converts and changes every hindrance to its activity into an aid; and so that which is a hindrance is made a furtherance to an act; and that which is an obstacle on the road helps us on this road (Book V: xx).

Be not ashamed to be helped; for it is your business to do your duty like a soldier in the assault on a town. How then, if being lame you cannot mount up on the battlements alone, but with the help of another it is possible? (Book VII: vii)

Not in passivity but in activity lie the evil and the good of the rational social being, just as his virtue and his vice lie not in passivity but in activity (Book IX: xvi).

My Meditations

1. Where have I experienced the support of other people in my professional and/or personal life?

2. What are the potential benefits to me if I serve others and allow myself to depend on them as well?

3. How can I practically implement this philosophy of living as an interdependent part of humanity?

DAY 41

Soon, very soon, you will be ashes, or a skeleton, and either a name or not even a name; but name is sound and echo. And the things which are much valued in life are empty and rotten and trifling, and like little dogs biting one another, and little children quarreling, laughing, and then straightway weeping. But fidelity and modesty and justice and truth are fled up to Olympus from the wide-spread earth (Book V: xxxiii).

Attend to the matter which is before you, whether it is an opinion or an act or a word. You suffer this justly, for you choose rather to become good tomorrow than to be good today (Book VIII: xxii).

Above, below, all around are the movements of the elements. But the motion of virtue is in none of these—it is something more divine, and advancing by a way hardly observed, it goes happily on its road (Book VI: xvii).

But as to what anyone will say or think about you or do against you, never even think of it, being contented with these two things—with acting justly in what you now do, and being satisfied with what is now assigned to you; and you lay aside all distracting and busy pursuits, and desire nothing else than to accomplish the straight course through the law and by accomplishing the straight course to follow God (Book X: xi).

My Meditations

1. Am I actively pursuing truth and goodness in my professional and/or personal life?

2. Do I really believe that things like honesty and justice are more important to me than anything else I can do today?

3. How can I act on my beliefs in this area?

DAY 42

A slave you are, Caesar. Free speech is not for you (Book XI: xxx).

As those who try to stand in your way when you are proceeding according to right reason will not be able to turn you aside from your proper action, so neither let them drive you from your benevolent feelings toward them, but be on your guard equally in both matters (Book XI: ix).

What is your art? To be good. And how is this accomplished well except by general principles, some about the nature of the universe, and others about the proper constitution of humanity? (Book XI: v)

Do what nature now requires. Set yourself in motion, if it is in your power, and do not look about you to see if anyone will observe it; nor yet expect Plato's Republic, but be content if the smallest thing goes on well, and consider such an event to be no small matter (Book IX: xxix).

Labor not as one who is wretched, nor yet as one who would be pitied or admired; but direct your will to one thing only—to put yourself in motion and to check yourself, as the social reason requires (Book IX: xii).

My Meditations

1. In my professional and/or personal life, how have I struggled in leadership? Are there tensions between "being myself" and being the leader others need me to be?

2. What are the potential benefits to me if I put others first in my leadership?

3. How can I practically implement this philosophy of servant-leadership?

DAY 43

Different things delight different people (Book VIII: xliii).

Another may be more expert in athletic skill; but he is not more social, nor more modest, nor better disciplined to meet all that happens, nor more considerate with respect to the faults of his neighbors (Book VII: lii).

When you wish to delight yourself, think of the virtues of those who live with you; for instance, the activity of one, and the modesty of another, and the liberality of a third, and some other good quality of a fourth. For nothing delights so much as the examples of the virtues, when they are exhibited in the morals of those who live with us and present themselves in abundance, as far as is possible. Therefore we must keep them before us (Book VI: xlviii).

The things from the gods deserve veneration for their excellence. The things from humanity should be dear to us by reason of kinship; and sometimes even, in a manner, they move our pity for people's ignorance of good and bad (Book II: xiii).

When you are offended with anyone's shameless conduct, immediately ask yourself, "Is it possible, then, that shameless people should not be in the world?" It is not possible. Do not, then, require what is impossible. For this person also is one of those shameless people who must of necessity be in the world. Let the same considerations be present to your mind in the case of the knave, and the faithless one, and of everyone who does wrong in any way (Book IX: xlii).

My Meditations

1. Who are the best people in my professional and/or personal life? Who seem like the worst people I know? Despite the obvious differences, can I see similarities between these people?

2. What are the potential benefits to me if I both delight in the best elements of humanity, but also forgive the failings I regularly encounter?

3. How can I practically implement this philosophy of embracing my kinship with the human race? Do I need to overcome some personal aversion to the idea of loving people whom I don't like?

DAY 44

You are formed by nature to bear everything, with respect to which it depends on your own opinion to make it endurable and tolerable, by thinking that it is either your interest or your duty to do this (Book X: iii).

Whatever may happen to you, it was prepared for you from all eternity; and the implication of causes was from eternity spinning the thread of your being, and of that which is incident to it (Book X: v).

That which the universal nature brings to each is for the good of each thing. And it is for its good at the time when nature brings it (Book X: xx).

If the gods have determined about me and about the things which must happen to me, they have determined well, for it is not easy even to imagine a deity without forethought; and as to doing me harm, why should they have any desire toward that? For what advantage would result to them from this, or to the whole, which is the special object of their providence? (Book VI: xliv)

The art of life is more like the wrestler's art than the dancer's, in respect of this, that it should stand ready and firm to meet onsets which are sudden and unexpected (Book VII: lxi).

My Meditations

1. In my professional and/or personal life, do I encounter things I don't think I can handle?

2. What are the potential benefits to me of taking a stoic view of events in my life? Can I perhaps handle more than I think I can?

3. How can I practically implement this philosophy of self-confidence?

DAY 45

It would be a person's happiest lot to depart from humankind without having had any taste of lying and hypocrisy and luxury and pride (Book IX: ii).

It is a base thing for the countenance to be obedient and to regulate and compose itself as the mind commands, and for the mind not to be regulated and composed by itself (Book VII: xxxvii).

In discourse you must attend to what is said, and in every movement you must observe what is doing. And in the one you should see immediately to what end it refers, but in the other watch carefully what is the thing signified (Book VII: iv).

One thing only troubles me, lest I should do something which the constitution of man does not allow, or in the way which it does not allow, or what it does not allow now (Book VII: xx).

The perfection of moral character consists in passing every day as the last, and in being neither violently excited nor torpid nor playing the hypocrite (Book VII: lxix).

My Meditations

1. Where have I experienced the deception of appearances in my professional and/or personal life?

2. Do I sometimes try to make myself seem better than I really am in some area? What are the potential benefits to me if I present myself with the same honesty as I would like others to use?

3. How can I practically implement this philosophy of consistency?

DAY 46

Constantly bring to your recollection those who have complained greatly about anything, those who have been most conspicuous by the greatest fame or misfortunes or enmities or fortunes of any kind; then think, "Where are they all now?" Smoke and ash and a tale, or not even a tale (Book XII: xxvii).

The words which were formerly familiar are now antiquated; so also the names of those who were famed of old are now in a manner antiquated. For all things soon pass away and become a mere tale, and complete oblivion soon buries them. And I say this of those who have shone in a wondrous way. For the rest, as soon as they have breathed out their breath they are gone, and no one speaks of them.

To conclude the matter, what is even an eternal remembrance? A mere nothing. What then is that about which we ought to employ our serious pains? This one thing—thoughts just, and acts social, and words which never lie, and a disposition which gladly accepts all that happens as necessary, as usual, as flowing from a principle and source of the same kind (Book IV: xxxiii).

What then is worth being valued? To be received with clapping of hands? No. Neither must we value the clapping of tongues; for the praise which comes from the many is a clapping of tongues. Suppose then that you have given up this worthless thing called fame, what remains that is worth valuing? To reverence and honor your own mind will make you content with yourself, and in harmony with society, and in agreement with the gods, that is, praising all that they give and have ordered (Book VI: xvi).

"Leaves, some the wind scatters on the ground—so is the race of men." Leaves, also, are your children; and leaves, too, are they who cry out as if they were worthy of credit and bestow their praise, or on the contrary curse, or secretly blame and sneer; and leaves, in like manner, are those who will receive and transmit your fame to after times (Book X: xxxiv).

My Meditations

1. Where have I been attracted by fame in my professional and/or personal life?

2. What are the potential benefits to me if I learn not to worry about public opinion?

3. How can I practically implement this philosophy?

DAY 47

The offenses which are committed through desire are more blamable than those which are committed through anger. For one who is excited by anger turns away from reason unconsciously; but one who offends through desire, being overpowered by pleasure, is more intemperate in their offences. One has been first wronged and, through pain, is compelled to be angry, but the other is moved by their own impulse to do wrong, being carried toward it by desire (Book II: x).

If you had a step-mother and a mother at the same time, you would be dutiful to your step-mother, but still you would constantly return to your mother. Let the court and philosophy now be to you step-mother and mother: return to philosophy frequently and repose in her (Book VI: xii).

We ought to consider that if a person should live longer, it is quite uncertain whether the understanding will still continue sufficient for the comprehension of things, and retain the power of contemplation. For if he shall begin to fall into dotage, the power of making use of ourselves, and filling up the measure of our duty, and considering whatever else absolutely requires a disciplined reason—all this is already extinguished. We must make haste, then, not only because we are daily nearer to death, but also because the conception of things and the understanding of them cease first (Book III: i).

Such as are your habitual thoughts, such also will be the character of your mind; for the soul is dyed by the thoughts. Dye it then with a continuous series of such thoughts as these: for instance, that where a person can live, there they can also live well.

But the things which have life are superior to those which have not life, and of those which have life the superior are those which have reason (Book V: xvi).

My Meditations

1. What is the role of reason in my professional and/or personal life?

2. In the modern era, we consider a person who acts on their emotions to be "true to themselves." This ancient view would say that acting based on anything other than reason is to act in a sub-human, animalistic way. What do I think about this?

3. How can I put into practice the level of value in which I hold rationalism versus emotionalism?

DAY 48

Wherever a person has placed themselves thinking it the best place for them, or has been placed by a commander, there in my opinion they ought to stay and to abide the hazard, taking nothing into the reckoning, either death or anything else, before the baseness of deserting their post (Book VII: xlv).

Let it make no difference to you whether you are cold or warm, if you are doing your duty; and whether you are drowsy or satisfied with sleep; and whether ill-spoken of or praised; and whether dying or doing something else. For it is one of the acts of life, this act by which we die; it is sufficient then in this act also to do well what we have in hand (Book VI: ii).

Direct your attention to what is said. Let your understanding enter into the things that are doing and the things which do them (Book VII: xxx).

When you rise from sleep with reluctance, remember that it is according to your constitution and according to human nature to perform social acts, but sleeping is common also to irrational beings (Book VIII: xii).

Neither in your actions be sluggish nor in your conversation without method, nor wandering in your thoughts, nor let there be in your soul inward contention nor external effusion, nor in life be so busy as to have no leisure (Book VIII: li).

My Meditations

1. Where have I made an effort to fulfill my obligations in my professional and/or personal life, regardless of what I would prefer to do?

2. What are the potential benefits to me if I finish every task before me as though it would be embarrassing to leave it unfinished?

3. How can I practically implement this philosophy of keeping my commitments?

DAY 49

You are not dissatisfied, I suppose, because you weigh only so many pounds and not three hundred. Be not dissatisfied then that you must live only so many years and not more; for as you are satisfied with the amount of substance which has been assigned to you, so be content with the time (Book VI: xlix).

If any god told you that you shall die tomorrow, or certainly on the day after tomorrow, you would not care much whether it was on the third day or on the morrow, unless you were in the highest degree mean-spirited; for how small is the difference! So think it no great thing to die after as many years as you can name rather than tomorrow (Book IV: xlvii).

No longer wander at random, for you will not read your own memoirs. Hasten to the end which you have before you, and, throwing away idle hopes, come to your own aid, if you care at all for yourself, while it is in your power (Book III: xiv).

Always observe how ephemeral and worthless human things are, and what was yesterday a little mucus, tomorrow will be a mummy or ashes. Pass then through this little space of time conformably to nature, and end your journey in content, as an olive falls off when it is ripe, blessing nature who produced it, and thanking the tree on which it grew (Book IV: xlviii).

My Meditations

1. Have I ever run out of time for something important in my professional and/or personal life?

2. What are the potential benefits to me if I keep my mortality present in my awareness?

3. How can I practically implement this philosophy of making the most of every day?

DAY 50

To look for the fig in winter is a madman's act. Such is the one who looks for their child when it is no longer a child (Book XI: xxxiii).

Every nature is contented with itself when it goes on its way well; and a rational nature goes on its way well when in its thoughts it assents to nothing false or uncertain, and when it directs its movements to social acts only, and when it confines its desires and aversions to the things which are in its power, and when it is satisfied with everything that is assigned to it by the common nature (Book VIII: vii).

For the stone which has been thrown up it is no evil to come down, nor indeed any good to have been carried up (Book IX: xvii).

It is not fit that I should give myself pain, for I have never intentionally given pain even to another (Book VIII: xlii).

My Meditations

1. Do I live consistent with the rhythms of nature in my professional and/or personal life?

2. What are the potential benefits to me if I do?

3. How can I practically implement this philosophy of accepting natural events as part of my life?

DAY 51

What is evil to you does not subsist in the ruling principle of another; nor yet in any turning and mutation of your corporeal covering. Where is it then? It is in that part of you in which subsists the power of forming opinions about evils. Let this power then not form such opinions, and all is well. Judge that nothing is either bad or good which can happen equally to the bad man and the good. For that which happens equally to him who lives contrary to nature and to him who lives according to nature is neither according to nature nor contrary to nature (Book IV: xxxix).

Things do not touch the soul, for they are external and remain immovable. Our perturbations come only from the opinion which is within. All these things, which you see, change immediately and will no longer be. Constantly bear in mind how many of these changes you have already witnessed. The universe is transformation—life is opinion (Book IV: iii).

It is in our power to have no opinion about a thing, and not to be disturbed in our soul; for things themselves have no natural power to form our judgments (Book VI: lii).

If this is neither my own badness, nor an effect of my own badness, and the common good is not injured, why am I troubled about it, and what is the harm to the common good? (Book V: xxxv)

Do not have such an opinion of things as the one who does you wrong, or such as they wish you to have, but look at things as they are in truth (Book IV: xi).

My Meditations

1. What do I think about the idea that "life is opinion"? Have I seen people who treat as truth something that is only their opinion? Do I ever do that?

2. What are the potential benefits to me if I reexamine my foundational beliefs?

3. What practical things should I do if I discover that some of the things I have been treating as universal truths are, in fact, basically just my opinions?

DAY 52

Think of the country mouse and of the town mouse, and of the alarm and trepidation of the town mouse (Book XI: xxii).

Imagine everyone who is grieved at anything or discontented to be like a pig which is sacrificed and kicks and screams (Book X: xxviii).

If a person is a stranger to the universe and does not know what is in it, no less is one a stranger who does not know what is going on in it. They are a runaway, who flies from social reason; they are blind, who shuts the eyes of understanding; they are poor, who has need of another, and has not all things which are useful for life. They are an abscess on the universe if they withdraw and separate from the reason of our common nature through being displeased with the things which happen. For the same nature produces this, and has produced you too. They are is a piece rent asunder from the state, who tears their own soul from that of reasonable beings, which is one (Book IV: xxix).

Always run to the short way; and the short way is the natural. Accordingly say and do everything in conformity with the soundest reason. For such a purpose frees a person from trouble, and warfare, and all artifice and ostentatious display (Book IV: li).

One who yields to pain and one who yields to anger, both are wounded and both submit (Book XI: xviii).

My Meditations

1. Where have I experienced worry in my professional and/or personal life?

2. What are the potential benefits of stoicism to me?

3. How can I practically implement this philosophy?

DAY 53

Such as bathing appears to you—oil, sweat, dirt, filthy water, all things disgusting—so is every part of life and everything (Book VIII: xxiv).

The rottenness of the matter which is the foundation of everything! Water, dust, bones, filth—or again, marble rocks, the callosities of the earth; and gold and silver, the sediments; and garments, only bits of hair; and purple dye, blood; and everything else is of the same kind. And that which is of the nature of breath is also another thing of the same kind, changing from this to that (Book IX: xxxvi).

Constantly contemplate the whole of time and the whole of substance, and consider that all individual things as to substance are a grain of a fig, and as to time the turning of a gimlet (Book X: xvii).

Tragedies were brought on the stage as means of reminding people of the things which happen to them, and that it is according to nature for things to happen so, and that, if you are delighted with what is shown on the stage, you should not be troubled with that which takes place on the larger stage (Book XI: vi).

In life the three acts are the whole drama; for what will be a complete drama is determined by the one who was once the cause of its composition, and now of its dissolution; but you are the cause of neither. Depart then satisfied, for he also who releases you is satisfied (Book XII: xxxvi).

My Meditations

1. Where have I been disillusioned with physical things in my professional and/or personal life?

2. What are the potential benefits to me of finding satisfaction in things that transcend the material world?

3. How can I practically implement this philosophy?

DAY 54

Love the art, poor as it may be, which you have learned, and be content with it; and pass through the rest of life like one who has entrusted to the gods with your whole soul all that you have, making yourself neither the tyrant nor the slave of anyone (Book IV: xxx).

What kind of things those are which appear good to the many, we may learn even from this. For if anyone should conceive certain things as being really good, such as prudence, temperance, justice, fortitude, they would not after having first conceived these endure to listen to anything which should not be in harmony with what is really good. But if a person has first conceived as good the things which appear to the many to be good, they will listen and readily receive as very applicable that which was said by the comic writer. Thus even the many perceive the difference (Book V: xii).

Reverence that which is best in the universe; and this is that which makes use of all things and directs all things. And in like manner also reverence that which is best in yourself; and this is of the same kind as that. For in yourself also, that which makes use of everything else is this, and your life is directed by this (Book V: xxi).

For the whole contains nothing which is not for its advantage; and all natures indeed have this common principle, but the nature of the universe has this principle besides, that it cannot be compelled even by any external cause to generate anything harmful to itself. I am a part of the whole which is governed by nature, and nothing is injurious to the part if it is for the advantage of the whole (Book X: vi).

My Meditations

1. Where have I undervalued myself and my abilities in my professional and/or personal life?

2. What are the potential benefits to me if I recognize myself as a valuable and necessary part of the whole?

3. How can I put practical action to my own sense of self-worth?

DAY 55

That which rules within is as fire which lays hold of what falls into it. A small light would be extinguished; but when the fire is strong, it soon appropriates to itself the matter which is heaped on it, and consumes it, and rises higher by means of this very material (Book IV: i).

All things come from that universal ruling power, either directly proceeding or by way of sequence. And accordingly the lion's gaping jaws, and that which is poisonous, and every harmful thing, as a thorn, as mud, are after-products of the grand and beautiful. Do not then imagine that they are of another kind from that which you do venerate, but form a just opinion of the source of all (Book VI: xxxvi).

The Pythagoreans bid us in the morning look to the heavens that we may be reminded of those bodies which continually do the same things and in the same manner perform their work, and also be reminded of their purity. For there is no veil over a star (Book XI: xxvii).

My Meditations

1. Where have I seen good triumphing over challenges in my professional and/or personal life? Do I believe that such a thing happens, or do I regard it as a fairy tale?

2. What are the potential benefits to me if I act as though the good things I am working toward are actually possible, despite all challenges?

3. How can I practically implement this philosophy of hope?

DAY 56

You have existed as a part. You shall disappear in that which produced you; but rather you shall be received back into its seminal principle by transmutation (Book IV: xiv).

I am composed of the formal and the material; and neither of them will perish into non-existence, as neither of them came into existence out of non-existence. Every part of me then will be reduced by change into some part of the universe, and that again will change into another part of the universe, and so on forever. And by consequence of such a change I too exist, and those who begot me, and so on forever in the other direction. For nothing hinders us from saying so, even if the universe is administered according to definite periods of revolution (Book V: xiii).

That which has died falls not out of the universe. If it stays here, it also changes here, and is dissolved into its proper parts, which are elements of the universe and of yourself. And these too change, and they murmur not (Book VIII: xviii).

My Meditations

1. What do I think about the idea that all things are part of one unified whole?

2. What are the potential benefits to me of living in my world as though it is all part of me, and I of it?

3. Whether or not I agree with this idea, how can I make practical use of it? Can I benefit from some of the attitudes expressed here?

DAY 57

Say nothing more to yourself than what the first appearances report. Suppose that it has been reported to you that a certain person speaks ill of you. This has been reported; but that you have been injured, that has not been reported. Thus then always abide by the first appearances, and add nothing yourself from within, and then nothing happens to you (Book VIII: xlix).

If we judge only those things which are in our power to be good or bad, there remains no reason either for finding fault with God or standing in a hostile attitude to others (Book VI: xli).

That which does not make a person worse than they were also does not make their life worse, nor does it harm them either from without or from within (Book IV: viii).

You will soon die, and you are not yet simple, nor free from perturbations, nor without suspicion of being hurt by external things, nor kindly disposed toward all; nor do you yet place wisdom only in acting justly (Book IV: xxxvii).

My Meditations

1. Where have I taken things too personally in my professional and/or personal life?

2. What are the potential benefits to me if I refuse to allow outside influences to harm me?

3. How can I practically implement this philosophy?

DAY 58

Either it is a well-arranged universe or a chaos huddled together, but still a universe. But can a certain order subsist in you, and disorder in the All? And this too when all things are so separated and diffused and sympathetic (Book IV: xxvii).

The substance of the universe is obedient and compliant; and the reason which governs it has in itself no cause for doing evil, for it has no malice, nor does it do evil to anything, nor is anything harmed by it. But all things are made and perfected according to this reason (Book VI: i).

How plain does it appear that there is not another condition of life so well suited for philosophizing as this in which you now happen to be (Book XI: vii).

My Meditations

1. Have I taken time in my life to examine the way the natural world works?

2. What are the potential benefits to me if I study some element of nature, as a hobby?

3. How can I practically implement this broader view of life to improve my own outlook?

DAY 59

Nothing harms a citizen which does not harm the state; nor yet does anything harm the state, which does not harm law order (Book X: xxxiii).

If a thing is in your own power, why do you do it? But if it is in the power of another, whom do you blame—the atoms chance or the gods? Both are foolish. You must blame nobody. For if you can, correct that which is the cause; but if you cannot do this, correct at least the thing itself; but if you cannot do even this, of what use is it to you to find fault? For nothing should be done without a purpose (Book VIII: xvii).

Reason and philosophy are powers which are sufficient for themselves and for their own works. They move then from a first principle which is their own, and they make their way to the end which is proposed to them. They proceed by the right road (Book V: xiv).

My Meditations

1. Where have I experienced good results from following reason in my professional and/or personal life?

2. What are the potential benefits to me if I focus on doing what I am able to do and don't worry about the rest?

3. How can I practically implement this philosophy for myself and those around me?

DAY 60

In everything which happens keep before your eyes those to whom the same things happened, and how they were vexed, and treated them as strange things, and found fault with them—and now where are they? Nowhere. Why then do you too choose to act in the same way? (Book VII: lviii)

One who fears death either fears the loss of sensation or a different kind of sensation. But if you shall have no sensation, neither will you feel any harm; and if you shall acquire another kind of sensation, you will be a different kind of living being and you will not cease to live (Book VIII: lviii).

With food and drinks and cunning magic arts turning the channel's course to escape from death. The breeze which heaven has sent we must endure, and toil without complaining (Book VII: li).

My Meditations

1. I have confronted the idea of death several times throughout this book. What is the overall effect on my professional and/or personal life?

2. Society likes to avoid this topic, considering it depressing. Is there a benefit to staying aware of death?

3. How can I practically implement the best ideas of stoic philosophy to improve my life?

THE *MEDITATIONS* OF MARCUS AURELIUS

Meditations is a series of personal writings by Marcus Aurelius, Roman Emperor from AD 161–180, recording his private notes to himself and ideas on Stoic philosophy. Aurelius was the last of the rulers later known as the Five Good Emperors and the last emperor of the *Pax Romana*, an age of relative peace, calm, and stability for the Roman Empire lasting from 27 BC to AD 180. He served as Roman consul before his reign as emperor.

The *Meditations* has been translated by numerous people throughout the centuries. This book takes excerpts from the 1862 edition translated by George Long (1800–1879), a widely known English writer and classical scholar. Some verbiage has been updated for modern readers.

ABOUT THE TRANSLATOR

George Long (1800 –1879) was an English writer and classical scholar. He is best known for his translations of the *Meditations* of Marcus Aurelius (1862) and the *Discourses of Epictetus* (1877). Alongside Charles Knight, he was the editor of the *Penny Cyclopaedia*, and he was widely known throughout England.

THANK YOU FOR READING THIS BOOK!

If you found any of the information helpful, please take a few minutes and leave a review on the bookselling platform of your choice.

BONUS GIFT!

Don't forget to sign up to try our newsletter and grab your free personal development ebook here:

soundwisdom.com/classics

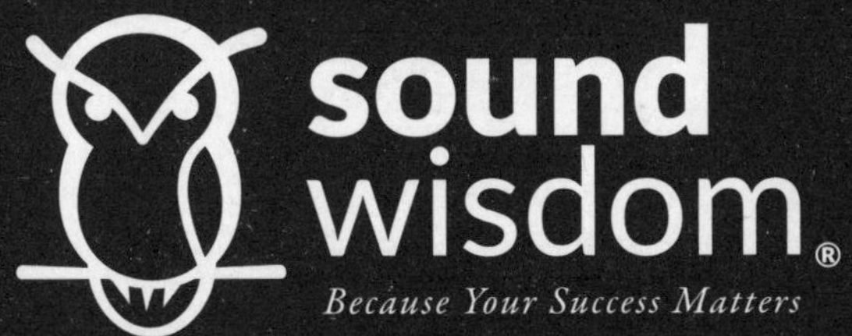